Broken Success

A teenage mother's journey through trauma and loss

Shawntae Bennett

The events and conversations in this book have been set down to the best of the author's ability, although some names and details have been changed to protect the privacy of individuals.

Copyright © 2026 by Shawntae Bennett

All rights reserved. No part of this book may be reproduced or used in any manner without written permission of the copyright owner except for the use of quotations in a book review.

First paperback edition January 2026
First ebook edition January 2026

ISBN 979-8-218-89948-6 (paperback)

Published by Shawntae Bennett

Dedication

Broken Success is dedicated to teenage mothers as a parable confirming Romans 8:18 (KJV): "For I reckon that the sufferings of this present time are not worthy to be compared with the glory which shall be revealed in us."

For every young mother who was told that her life was over — this is proof it was just beginning.

Acknowledgments

To my mom—thank you for making me successful. Your words and actions prepared me for life as a black woman living in America. I pray that now that we are both mothers, we can mend our relationship. A special toast to our good days outweighing our bad days.

To my dad—thank you for making me broken. Losing you at such a vulnerable age keeps me humble. Missing you keeps me considerate and Christ-like. I pray your presence surrounds me daily.

To my daughter—thank you for saving me. Being your mother gives me purpose and passion. You are evidence that broken translates to beautiful.

To my siblings—thank y'all for working my nerves. We all have different personalities, yet we manage to love and lift each other up.

I love y'all forever and always.

To my sister-friends—many see us in photos at dinners, parties, and vacations, but what many have not seen is you guys being my life jackets through troubled waters. Thank y'all for always riding for me from dusk to dawn.

To my writing coach, Tyneisha Reed—thank you for being my midwife. Your guidance made the labor and joy of *Broken Success* possible. May the good Lord continue to bless you and everything attached to you.

Table of Contents

Foreward	1
Chapter 1: Foundations	4
Chapter 2: Roar	14
Chapter 3: The First Shock	22
Chapter 4: Carrying the Weight	32
Chapter 5: Labor of Love	38
Chapter 6: Young Motherhood	47
Chapter 7: Sisterhood	56
Chapter 8: Sweet 16	62
Chapter 9: Rising Higher	71
Chapter 10: Healing the Girl, Guiding the Mother	78
Chapter 11: Raising a Teen	87
Chapter 12: Success	98
Chapter 13: Full Circle	107
Picture Gallery	114
Author Bio	117

Foreword

I would like to take this time to congratulate my sister for staying true to her goals and her purpose throughout her life. Her determination and resilience have always been a source of inspiration to me, whether she realizes it or not. She has continuously shown what it means to stand firm in faith and to keep pushing forward, even when the odds seem stacked against her. Watching her journey has not only been motivating—it has been life-changing.

Regardless of what we went through growing up as inner-city kids in Charleston, South Carolina, she never let our circumstances define her. She stayed the course, holding tight to her dreams even when the path wasn't easy or clear. From a young age, she knew what she wanted to be—a teacher—and she pursued that dream with a passion that never faded. I can still remember us as kids, sitting in our room, pretending to be in class, with her acting as the teacher and me as the student. I would always get in "trouble" and end up with detention, which, looking back, was quite fitting since I was a bit of a handful. But even then, I could see the spark in her—her patience, her creativity, and her love for helping others learn.

Growing up wasn't always easy. Life was bittersweet—never all good, never all bad—but we had each other, and that made all the difference. No matter what life threw our way, we stuck together. We looked out for each other and found ways to keep moving forward. I'm sure this book will tell many of those stories in great detail — the laughter, the tears, the struggles, and the triumphs that shaped who she is today.

I'm beyond excited to finally read this book. Knowing my sister, I can already tell it will touch hearts, open minds, and bring out every emotion known to man. Her words are thoughtful and carefully crafted, filled with meaning, honesty, and depth. This book not only tells her story, but also speaks to anyone who has faced challenges, doubted themselves, or wondered if they could rise above their circumstances. It will remind readers that strength isn't about perfection — it's about perseverance, faith, and love.

Through every challenge, setback, and victory, my sister has continued to evolve into the remarkable woman she is today — a loving sister, a dedicated teacher, a devoted mother, and a woman of purpose. She carries herself with grace, speaks with wisdom, and moves with intention. Her story is not just her own — it belongs to every person who has ever dared to dream beyond their environment and believed that something greater awaited them.

I truly believe that this book will not only inspire those who read it but will also leave a lasting impact on everyone who knows her. It's a reflection of her journey, her heart, and her unwavering belief that dreams are worth chasing. And with all that she's accomplished and all that's still to come, I have no doubt that one day, the title of *New York Times* bestselling author will be added to her long list of achievements.

With love and admiration,
Triverio Bennett

Chapter 1

Foundations

Long before I ever decided to have a child, I promised myself I would never love a man. Releasing that kind of power made women weak and bitter, and I would *never* be weak or bitter. Love seemed so temporary. How could two people create children together yet end up at war with one another?

One Saturday morning, Mom was getting ready for work, and my older brother and I were cleaning the house. Mom called us over to the kitchen in a low whisper. My heart pounded in my chest. What bad thing had happened? That was the only time my mom used that low tone. Pointing to the newspaper, Mom said, "Y'all dad went to jail. I just wanted to tell y'all before y'all heard it from someone else."

My older brother and I locked eyes and, in sync, walked back to the living room to clean. Once my mom left for work, we ran back to the kitchen to read the newspaper, but the newspaper was gone. "How long do you think Dad is going to be in jail for?" I asked.

"I'm not sure, but someone will tell me at the park later."

My mom hated my dad. If you ever mentioned his name in her presence, you would know right away. "A deadbeat dad creating broken homes every chance he gets," she would say. "Don't pay any attention to the first two he made."

This dynamic made it hard to feel loved by both parents. I spent a lot of time trying to figure out which parent was the good parent. I wanted to know if the things my mom said about my dad were true. Dad never said anything about my mom, good or bad. I guess that was his protection from the chaos they had created.

When I was under five years old, we moved to Bayside Manor Apartments, a government project publicized as one of the most dangerous places to live in Charleston, South Carolina. Growing up, we always specified that we lived in Bayside Manor: the back portion of the complex, not the front, known as Bayside Gardens. You had to pass cemeteries on both sides of the road coming through the back entrance. We would turn the music off as we were told noise would awaken the dead. Bayside's most unique characteristic was the orange hallways. Every few years, management would paint the exterior different colors, yet the chipped orange hallways stayed the same. Bayside Manor was home not only to me, my mom, and my brothers, but also to two of my grand-aunts and a host of cousins from both my mom's and dad's sides of the family.

Kids rode their bikes, ran around the playground, and played jump rope and hand games like Ms. Mary Mack around Bayside Manor all day. My favorite was when my older brother toted me around on the handlebars of his bike. We went on "missions" to the Star service station, safely crossing a major highway to buy chips, juice, and Frooties candy.

We even had a dance and basketball team that competed against other neighborhoods. When kids weren't spread all over the complex, we were gathering at the community center out back. This center hosted my first talent show, where I sang "I Believe I Can Fly" by R. Kelly. I was so nervous I forgot one of the verses, but the audience still clapped for me. The center also hosted spelling bees and homework help and often gave rewards for good grades on report cards.

And if we weren't doing any of that, we were fighting one another. Pulling hair, punching, and stomping on each other for reasons I cannot recall anymore. Some days, I was on top, and other days, I was in the dirt. The craziest part was how we would all be friends again the following day. We played all day but had to be home before the streetlights came on. At nightfall, the adults hung out in the yards, eating crabs, drinking beer, and listening to music. Nighttime could also get dangerous. Large fights would break out, or gunfire would erupt. One night, my mother's car got stolen when she left it running to race upstairs to grab something.

Bayside was the first place I experienced snow. School was canceled, and my older brother and I made snowmen and threw snowballs at one another. This level of excitement wasn't experienced again until my tenth birthday. That year, my mom allowed me to have a birthday party in our apartment. The living room was filled wall to wall with all the neighborhood kids dancing to the latest songs. Parents were out on the front lawn, so we partied past dark without any disruptions. My birthday party was the talk of Bayside for months to come.

My eleventh birthday was memorable for entirely an different reason. Just short of my birthday, we got evicted due to some activities my older brother was involved in.

I refused to pack when my mom told me we had to leave. I hoped something would change, that we could suddenly stay. Then one day, my mom busted in my bedroom door. She threw a sixteen-pack of large black trash bags on my bed, yelling, "Shawntae, pack this got damn room or everything is going in the trash. I already told your ass we have to be out next week. This is not the time to be bullshitting around."

My mother's use of profanity told me she meant every word. It was time to get my act together. I packed my entire room in one night with the song "Missing You" from the *Set It Off* movie soundtrack playing on repeat. I slept in my closet that night. A small act of rebellion. Mom hated me lying on the carpet because it would trigger my asthma.

My mom couldn't find a place right away, so we went to live with a friend of hers for a while. A year and several disappointments later, we finally got our own place again, on Butler Street. During that time, my mom had transitioned into the bail bondsman business. She liked doing administrative work and meeting new people, so this new job brought her joy. But when she got into the business, I doubt she expected it to help my father out. She sat my brother and me down one Thursday afternoon after school and said, "Your father contacted me, asking for my help getting out of jail."

My brother and I glanced at each other, and my whole body clenched. Conversations about my father never went well.

"I don't want to help him. He deserves to sit in there after what he did. But I'm gonna do it anyway. For y'all, not him, so y'all can see him."

Days later, when I came home from school, there he was, sitting on our downstairs sofa. I screamed and threw myself into his arms. He hugged me tightly and spun around. Tears streamed down my face. "I missed you, Dad."

"Me too, baby, me too. It's so good to see you."

In the months to come, Dad was around a lot more. He would pick my brothers and me up from school. Or he would come pick up my older brother, who was escaping a butt-whooping from my mom. I would stay awake late on the weekends when my mom went to the nightclub to hear her gossip on the phone about seeing my dad at the club. "I can't believe he is in the club buying drinks like he doesn't owe me child support."

About seven months after my dad's release, my mom was laid off from her job due to budget cuts. It was time for a major transition, a gut-wrenching change. Mom divided up her kids to different family members: I went with my cousin, Dawn, my older brother went with Uncle Anthony, and my younger brother went with our grand-aunt, Dorthey. My mother moved many miles away to Florida, attempting to get herself settled before moving us to Florida with her. We had visited Florida a few times before, including a trip to Disney World, but moving there was not on my radar. But after that, I didn't care where we lived as long as I was under the same roof with my mom and brothers again. It was the first time I hadn't lived with them.

Loneliness crept in. Even though I was surrounded by familiar faces, my heart ached for my mom and my brothers. I would cry myself to sleep every night. The phone calls between us were always too brief and left me heartbroken. My two cousins would try to cheer me up, going out shopping or for ice cream. But nothing worked. My adult cousin, a hairstylist, kept my hair nice. I was loved and well-cared for, but it wasn't the same. Nothing could make up for their absence in my life.

My mom must have needed to see us too, because she randomly came up to Charleston for a visit; either that, or things weren't working in Florida, and she didn't want to tell us. One thing I do know is that I was glad to be in the same space with my mom and brothers again. I threw myself in their arms and wept until I could hardly breathe. I was so happy to be with them again, I didn't even care that we were sleeping in my grandfather's run-down trailer. He hadn't even cleaned out the cabinets since my grandmother passed away six years prior.

It was a Friday night, and I opted to sleep in the master bedroom with my mom. In those days, I was under my mom's feet every chance I had. I had just celebrated my twelfth birthday weeks prior, so I showered my mom with thanks for allowing me to get a second ear piercing. I dozed off for a short while before I slowly awoke to my mom's whispers. Since before I could remember, I always had a bad habit of eavesdropping on my mom's calls, and that night was no different. I kept my eyes closed but my ears open.

"Girl, what happened?" my mom asked.

"Verio got shot," her friend said.

"Where? Is he okay?"

"No, he died in his car."

My heart dropped to my stomach.

"Dead? How am I going to tell my kids he's dead?"

A warm waterfall of tears rolled down my cheeks. How could my father be *dead*? Who would want to hurt my dad?

The Post & Courier newspaper talked all about him, but no one ever figured out who was responsible for taking his life.

My mom stayed in Charleston. We spent the next few months living in the trailer, but this time, we didn't feel like a family. Distance stretched between us. We kept to ourselves, talking only about essential stuff. My mom was quieter than I remembered her, less confrontational. My older brother spent most of his time working to earn money with our older cousins. My younger brother spent a lot of time playing out in the yard with the dogs.

I isolated myself in my room, listening to music and reading books until nightfall, when I would cry myself to sleep. Spiritually, I broke in half when my dad passed. One side was the happy girl with fond memories of her dad, while the other side was hopeless, longing to know what would become of her life now that she was fatherless. There was a hole in me, and as far as I knew, everyone could see it. I felt like a can that had been dropped, so dented everywhere the store placed the can on clearance.

Just like that can, I became a reduced version of my old self.

I was powerful when I had a dad. But that power turned to weakness when he died. I was confident when I had a dad, but my confidence turned to confusion when he died. My dad's death broke my spirit, but I was too young to understand the impact that would have on my life. I was hurting in ways I didn't know how to name, and I kept it all locked inside. I started building the belief that only bad things happened to girls like me — girls with no dad to stand behind them. It was a lie, but I was too broken to know better. I didn't realize then how long it would take to unlearn that, or how deeply it would shape the girl I was becoming.

Reflection: A broken foundation doesn't mean you can't build a strong future. For a long time, I believed my family history defined the limits of who I could become, as if the pain I inherited was the only thing I had to offer the world. But looking back, I can see how those cracks taught me to stand on my own feet, to pay attention to what I wanted to carry forward and what I needed to leave behind. My past shaped me, yes, but it didn't seal my fate. If anything, it pushed me to imagine a future sturdier than I came from.

Writing Prompt: Write about a moment when your family history shaped how you saw yourself. How did it change your views and beliefs? How did those new views and beliefs affect your life going forward?

Broken Success

Shawntae Bennett

Chapter 2

Roar

I was born with a voice so loud that every time I talked, people accused me of yelling.

In 2001, Mom put us in better schools in North Charleston. But I was nervous. At my old school, the majority of students looked like me, but I would be the minority at this new school, and I feared being stereotyped. But I was also hopeful that this fresh start would be good for me, a second chance to get things right — I had been removed from school during the last few days for hitting a teacher. It wasn't even intentional, just an accident blown out of proportion and reported by a bystander. My teacher didn't have the courage to tell the whole truth. I took my punishment in silence since I already had a bad reputation of being a fighter.

At this new school, I wanted to make good grades and stay out of trouble, but I quickly learned that *wanting* to stay out of trouble and *staying* out of trouble were two different things, especially when my older brother attended the same school.

One Wednesday afternoon, we were waiting to get picked up from school. My mom was running late, and my brother was running his mouth with his classmate. Within the blink of an eye, my brother's beef quickly became mine. They didn't want to fight. Instead, they bet whose sister could beat who up. I prayed my mom would hurry up and get there, but it didn't happen fast enough. As soon as Tasha got within a foot of my personal space, it turned into hammer time. Survival mode reared up. My hands grew sweaty, and my heart raced. I knew what I had to do, whether I wanted to do it or not.

Good thing for me, it was so late after school that not many people saw me become the Tasmanian Devil's little sister, protecting my new "quiet girl" image.

But it wasn't long before a boy nicknamed Big D was picking on me. As an adult, I understand that he likely had a crush on me and pulled my hair because that's what boys do at that age, but at that time, all I knew was that someone was pulling my hair, so he needed to get beat down. I treated the classroom like it was *WWE SmackDown* and I was China — I had Big D stretched out across the small groups' table. That incident led to my first suspension in my new school. The whole class laughed, but I was disappointed in myself. I had fallen back into my old ways and let myself down. I proved all the naysayers right instead of wrong. That was one of the longest walks to the office I had ever taken.

Humiliated and ashamed to tell my mother, I played sick for three days to stay home. My mother already viewed me as a burden, and telling her would have only added to it. I made a vow to never fight at school again because this new school had strict consequences.

But that vow did not transfer over to the neighborhood. Within a week of being suspended from school, I beat a girl up on Range Drive as I waited for the Carter City bus to take me home. This girl actually had a knife in her possession that I had to wrestle away from her as she tried to slice my face. My name made waves around the school and community. People were ready to see me finally lose a fight. They would get their wish the day I went toe to toe with the school resource officer (SRO).

My anger began when the SRO joked about me potentially getting sick from eating pork that sat in my backpack for hours. In tough, sassy girl fashion, I walked up and stood face to face with the SRO. "Don't concern yourself with what I'm putting in my mouth."

In the middle of the cafeteria, she pulled my hands behind my back, kicked my knees inward, and smashed my face onto the table in one smooth move. The cafeteria's noisy chatter silenced. A wave of powerlessness and shame washed over me. Being slammed like that didn't just hurt; it exposed me. It made me look wild, out of control — a label I never wanted. I couldn't process what had happened until I was handcuffed in the back of the police cruiser. Looking out the back window of that police cruiser, regret and confusion simmered. How on Earth was I going to get myself out of this?

But instead of taking me to the juvenile detention center for troubled youth, the officer took me to my mother, a bail bondsman located across the street from the county jail.

I spent the day watching families bring in money and paperwork for their loved ones to be released. I listened as former inmates got released and discussed the horrible conditions in the jail and swore never to go back. Then a woman named Cynthia came in to talk with my mom and her coworkers. She explained that she didn't know where else to go after leaving the courts because both her parents were deceased, and her older brother was the only family she had left. Apparently, her brother kept the company in business with his need for bail-bonds. But not anymore. Her brother had been sentenced to life in prison for killing his girlfriend. Clyde didn't intentionally kill his girl; they got into an argument that led to a physical fight, and one of Clyde's blows ended Kim's life. Clyde had a long rap sheet that allowed the state to give him the maximum sentence for his charge.

My mom told Cynthia about the incident from school, so she pulled me close and started to minister to me about my actions. I told her about the fights my mom didn't know about. I told her how I wanted to change, but didn't know how. She said, "You're a born leader. You'll need to decide whether you're going to lead your people to destruction or prosperity."

I tossed and turned all night thinking of my encounter with Cynthia. Reality hit me. Cynthia's pained cries made me think about my choices more closely. I didn't want my siblings crying for me like that while I sat in a jail cell.

When I went back to school the following week, I was determined to avoid addressing any negativity. The first day back was the worst. Students and staff stared at me like I was a wild animal. By day two, the drama started back up. Jasmine told me that Shelly wanted to fight me because her sister Shanelle said I rolled my eyes at her weeks ago. I told Jasmine I had done enough and I was not fighting anymore.

Recess time came, and Shelly ran her mouth about how she had waited for me to return to school so she could clear up the issues with her sister and me. Every word she threw at me felt like a dare, a tug back toward the girl I used to be. I wanted to snap, but instead, I put my head down and remained silent. That small act felt like lifting a weight no one else could see. Within minutes, Shelly stopped yelling, and the crowd lost interest, drifting away in search of new entertainment. When my teacher arrived to take us back to class, I made sure I was the first in line—not because I was scared, but because I was choosing something different for myself.

In the restroom, I finally let the pressure spill over. I cried quietly, releasing all the anger and frustration I had held inside. Fighting the urge to fight was its own kind of battle, and it drained me. But even through the tears, I felt a flicker of pride. Change wasn't easy, especially when people expected me to stay the same, but at that moment, I had chosen growth. I washed my face, breathed deep, and headed back to class to do my work, carrying the small but strong seed of a new version of myself. For the next few weeks, I was as quiet as a mouse, focusing on schoolwork, chores at home, and reading.

Then my favorite teacher, Coach Trip, was absent one day, and we had a substitute. I was nervous because most people viewed PE as free play, and unstructured activities often led to drama, which led to fights. Out of survival mode, I decided to be Coach for the day. Keeping busy was the only strategy I had to avoid trouble.

I yelled for the five grade classes to line up, and I walked us through the warm-up session. Then, into rounds of girls versus boys dodgeball games. Everyone listened and participated, and there were zero fights. The substitute gave compliment, to my teacher about my actions. That day, I learned that my voice could lead. I learned that a roar should be used to give instruction or to express emotions, not to spread useless information or to hurt others. My roar grew up, less fists, more focus. Less noise, more power.

Reflection: A roar isn't always loud—sometimes it's choosing silence. That day I chose not to fight, I didn't just find my voice, I found my purpose.

Writing Prompt: Write about a time you had to channel your anger into growth. What angered you? How did you soothe yourself? What did this process teach you about yourself and others?

Broken Success

Shawntae Bennett

Chapter 3

The First Shock

"Have you gotten your period yet?" my boyfriend Tony asked.

I chewed on my lip hard enough that I tasted blood. "Nope."

"You think you pregnant?" He paced the room, running his hands over his hair.

Taking a deep breath, I wiped my tears before they fell, then whispered, "I don't know."

He drove me to Walgreens. I went into the store, grabbed a pregnancy test, and went straight to the restroom to take it. The smell of fresh Clorox overpowered me. The workers tried to make the gloomy old bathroom appear clean by using way too much bleach.

My focus shifted from where I was to the reason I was there. My hands trembled as I opened the box and pulled the test out. The words on the instruction sheet blurred as I tried to read them. After several calming breaths and a few more tears, I finally managed to take the test. Then I waited the longest three minutes of my life.

I checked my watch over and over, praying the test was negative. I couldn't even take care of myself. How could I take care of a baby? The second the three minutes were up, I turned the test over.

There they were. Two dark pink lines.

My breath caught in my throat, and I sat there with my head in my hands for several long minutes, flashing through every emotion—panic, fear, joy, anxiety, determination. I should have known I was pregnant because I had to pee more than usual these past few months. My brain swarmed with thoughts, but my body was frozen in disbelief.

I was about to become someone's mother!

I walked out of the restroom and handed the positive test to Tony. He said, "I knew you was pregnant. I hope it's a girl," and back to the car we went.

On the way back home, we stopped by Popeyes for some chicken. He ordered our usual chicken meal with biscuits, red beans, and rice. We were both living at a hotel at that point, and once we arrived in the hotel parking lot, our hangout when both of our hotel rooms had people in them, he prepared the food by crushing the biscuit into the rice. The smell of fried chicken usually made my stomach growl, but this time, it made me sick.

Tony ate in silence, tearing into the red beans and rice like nothing had changed. But *everything* had changed. I stared out the window, watching people laugh and walk by, thinking about how my world had just tilted.

I was still trying to understand how in the heck I was pregnant. Though I wasn't a dumb girl, I wasn't sexually smart. I knew babies came from men and women having sex, but I was not a woman. I was a young girl who had no idea how her own body worked. No one told me that having a period indicated that my body could become pregnant. Confused and ashamed, I worried I would get in trouble for something I didn't understand.

"When are you going to tell your mama so we can see a doctor?" Tony asked, breaking the silence.

"I don't know." How would I even explain this to her?

"Don't take too long."

I rehearsed the words "I'm pregnant" for four days before gathering the courage to tell my mom. Each night, I lay in bed, examining every possible outcome. In one version, she hugged me. In another, she screamed. Mostly, I just pictured her face turning blank, the same way it did whenever anything disappointed her. The secret sat on my chest like a stone I couldn't lift.

I talked to myself every day. "Shawntae, it is now or never. Shawntae, you cannot hide forever." I planned to tell my mom when she first got home from work, so it would just be her and me in the room. But that night, I saw a black cat. Black cats brought bad luck, or so the superstition said, and I almost gave in to it and didn't tell her, but I had no choice.

Those ten stairs to our room felt like a hundred. I second-guessed telling my mom with every step I climbed. But I couldn't hide this forever.

My mom was listening to the news on TV while she unpacked her lunchbox from work. My heart thundered in my chest, hands shaking so hard I had to squeeze them into fists. I took the final step into the kitchen. "Mom, can I talk to you for a minute?"

She turned toward me in slow motion because of the strange tone of my voice or the fact that we no longer had emotional conversations. My mom looked me dead in my eyes, giving me her undivided attention. I cleared my throat and looked away. Disappointment would surely flash across her face, and I couldn't bear to see it yet.

"I need to tell you something."

"What?" She propped her hands on her hips.

I stepped to the table and gripped the back of a chair so hard my knuckles paled. "I'm pregnant."

Silence. Long enough that I finally had to look at her.

"How do you know?"

"I took a test, and it came out positive."

She shook her hand and tossed a Tupperware container into the sink. "I knew that already."

Her words hit harder than any slap. I thought I was about to drop a bomb, but she already saw the smoke. Part of me was relieved she didn't yell, but the other part felt invisible, like I'd been screaming without sound all this time.

"I noticed you weren't using any pads for months now. Plus, that nurse at your school was hinting at you being pregnant, but I shut that down. How far along are you?"

"A few months."

You don't know exactly?"

"I have it written in my diary."

"Go get the diary."

Relief flooded me as I walked to my diary and flipped back to that entry. "Here, I wrote my last period was in May."

"So, you already about six months?"

"I guess."

Mom started cutting vegetables for dinner. "Who the daddy?"

I winced. "Tony."

"Tony? That boy you been sneaking talking to?"

"Yes."

As we talked, my sense of relief over getting the words out was overshadowed by the fact that my mom knew already. My mom had failed me. She hadn't taught me about my body, and instead of addressing her suspicions, she had remained quiet. Not only was I preparing to be a mother at such a young age, but I only had three months left to do so before the baby arrived. I hadn't seen a doctor for the first six months of my pregnancy. What if something was wrong?

The phone rang, interrupting my thoughts. I was hoping it was someone who would take the attention off me, but I knew I was wrong when my mother handed me the phone.

"Hello?"

"Is it him?" my mom asked.

I nodded. Tony had called to check on me.

"Where is he at? I need to meet him. Tell him to come over here right now."

In an uncertain voice, I repeated my mom's demands to him. I could tell Tony was a little nervous because he asked me questions, attempting to read the energy in the room. "She wants me to come over there now?"

"Yeah."

"You think I should? Is she mad?"

"Not really. I don't know, just come over now."

"Are you okay?"

"Yes."

I kept glancing at the window, hoping headlights would flash across the curtains. But Tony never came. My brothers' footsteps filled the silence he left. They kept peering into the kitchen, then walking away. "Go head and tell them," Mom said.

My older brother didn't say a word, but his jaw tightened. He didn't have to speak for me to know he was angry — at the world for making me grow up too fast and at the responsibility of helping me care for the baby.

My younger brother wanted details. "Where's the baby?"

I showed him my belly.

"Is it a boy or girl?"

"I don't know yet."

At eight years old, he was super excited and ready to meet this baby. At least someone was. Mom allowed me to sleep in the bed with her since it was confirmed I was with child, while my brothers slept on the pull-out couch.

Once I told my mother I was pregnant, Mother Nature hit the set-free button. I was always a big-boned girl, so it hadn't been noticeable before. But now that I had confirmed my pregnancy, I woke up the next day with the roundest belly. My belly button poked out, and a dark black line ran down the center of my stomach.

But I could not imagine bringing a life into this world. I just wanted this baby to go away and come back to me later in life, when I was older, with more resources. Too late.

How would I finish school? How would I get a good job to support this child? What would everyone else say when they found out? The questions piled up so fast I could hardly breathe. I felt like the whole world was closing in on me, waiting for me to fail before I even began. I was still a kid myself, trying to figure out who I was, and suddenly, I was responsible for a life I didn't know how to protect. Every fear I'd ever had about my future rushed to the surface, and all I could think was that I wasn't ready—not for this, not for any of it.

I promised my baby that I would do everything possible to tend to her/his every need. And I promised myself that even though I was fatherless and a baby having a baby, that I would not pass down my traumas to my offspring.

As the room went quiet, I placed my hand over my stomach and whispered, "I don't know who I'll become, but please, help me love whoever you are."

I didn't know it then, but that was my first real prayer as a mother.

Reflection: That moment felt like an ending, but it was the beginning of my greatest role. I didn't know it then—how could I?—but the fear I felt that day would one day be replaced with a strength I didn't even know I had. What started as a shock became the doorway to a version of myself I never imagined I could grow into.

Writing Prompt: Write about a moment when unexpected news changed your life forever, when everything shifted in an instant, and you had to decide what to carry forward and what to leave behind.

Shawntae Bennett

Chapter 4
Carrying the Weight

"Excuse me, young lady, are you pregnant?"

I froze, staring at her badge instead of her eyes. Her voice was gentle, but my heart was pounding so loud I could barely hear her. No one had ever said the word out loud to me before. It felt strange hearing "pregnant," like it belonged to someone older, not me.

"Yes."

"Well, tomorrow is the day before spring break, and you know the kids get rowdy. Stay home. I'll have the counselor reach out to your family to discuss your schooling options for the remainder of your pregnancy and after birth."

Dean Brown was the first one at school to notice that I was pregnant, literally five days before my due date. By the time I was in eighth grade and pregnant, I had mastered the skill of not being seen or heard. I disappeared in plain sight, hoodie up, backpack across my stomach, headphones on even when the music wasn't playing. I didn't want anyone to see the changes in my body or the fear in my eyes. My silence became my safety blanket. I had given myself an assigned seat in every class and did every assignment with perfection. Anything to keep the teachers from looking too closely. When I finished my assignments, I would take a nap until the next period.

My teachers didn't find out that I was pregnant until I had delivered my daughter and was out of school on maternity leave. According to the school counselor, they were all shocked.

"We cannot believe she was balancing school and pregnancy so well."

Not even Mrs. Hunt suspected the day I experienced morning sickness in her class.

"Mrs. Hunt, may I please go to the restroom?"

"Yes, after we're done reading page thirteen."

Before my classmate reached the third line of the passage, I vomited on page thirteen.

The room went silent. The smell of acid and paper mixed together. I could feel everyone's eyes on me. I wanted to disappear into page thirteen.

My legs felt weak, but I forced myself to walk out of the classroom with what little pride I had left.

The nurse asked me what I had eaten.

"A burger for dinner, but I didn't eat breakfast."

She gave me some Saltine crackers and orange juice, which gave me some energy and calmed my stomach. I lay down until the nurse told me to go to lunch, but I ended up back there again because I vomited the pepperoni pizza I had eaten.

I stayed home the next few days, upset because I was already missing days and school had just started. I stayed away from the pizza for the next few weeks and only ate chicken sandwiches and fruit and drank chocolate milk. This seemed to do the trick. No more vomiting.

All I wanted to eat at home was burgers, and living across the street from McDonald's was a match made in heaven. The workers knew my order before I opened my mouth. Sometimes, I'd sit in the corner booth, rubbing my belly and pretending everything was normal. That burger and fries were the only things that didn't judge me; they just filled the emptiness I couldn't explain. My favorite was a quarter-pounder with cheese, fries, and an Oreo McFlurry.

The emptiness came from the lack of support, the lack of care others showed me, especially my family. "Shawntae, don't be coming in this room doing all that yelling no more, huh? She was talking about how she wanted y'all to clean up before I got home, so she didn't have to hear me yell. But the truth is, she was doing all that yelling because she was hiding that baby. All that guilt made her angry. Now that the world knows she's pregnant, she gets to relax and don't have to do all that yelling."

I stood there in the bathroom, frozen, listening. The shock hit me in the chest first, hard and sudden, like that drop on a roller coaster right before it takes off. I held my breath, not wanting to miss a single word. Each sentence felt like another crack forming inside me. Anger burned under my skin, but so did something quieter — a familiar sense of being outnumbered. It was always the two of them against me, and I knew confronting them would only end the same way it always did. So I stayed hidden, swallowing the hurt, letting the walls catch the tears I wasn't allowed to show.

My mom and older brother talked about me being pregnant and how they interpreted my behavior change. Calls came in from Charleston about my pregnancy, and everyone wanted to know my plans. Most said things like: "Do you really think you can handle that? You're too young for all that responsibility. You should've thought about this before. That's going to be a lot harder than you think. You can't raise a baby on hope alone."

I learned the less I said, the less I had to prove, so I kept all my responses short and sweet. I knew I would beat the odds. So, I just allowed them to gossip.

Shawntae is so loud. Shawntae yells a lot. Shawntae fat. Shawntae is always fighting. Shawntae always has something to say. Shawntae always wants something her way. Shawntae is too black. Shawntae lost a lot of weight. Shawntae, are you smoking crack? Shawntae, the year you were born was the worst year of my life. Shawntae, how old are you? Shawntae, you don't look like you should have a daughter that old. I had heard so many negative things about myself leading up to that point that I was numb to it all. Nothing nobody said would make me lose focus on being a good mother to my child. You damned if you do, and you damned if you don't!

Reflection: Carrying life while being judged taught me strength that no classroom could.

Writing Prompt: Describe a season when you carried more than you thought you could handle.

Broken Success

Chapter 5

Labor of Love

On March 15, the sun was warm on my skin, and for a few hours, I forgot that I was about to be a mother. My friends and I laughed about spring break plans and what movies we wanted to see. We hung around the complex and went for a nice swim in the pool. I was still living the version of myself who was free.

At ten p.m., just after my shower, the sharpest pain of my life slammed through me. Deep and unfamiliar, like my bones were folding inward. It started at the right side of my belly and raced left, up, and down in a matter of seconds.

Contractions.

I tried to breathe like I'd seen on TV, but all I could think was, *It's happening. I'm not ready.*

I grabbed my baby bag and called for my mom, and she took me to Arnold Palmer Hospital. When I arrived, the hospital room buzzed with energy. Nurses moved around me like I was invisible and urgent at the same time. My mother's face was calm, but her hands shook. I wanted to ask if she was scared too, but another contraction ripped through me before I could speak.

"Who is your OBGYN? How many weeks are you?"

"Ms. Nurse, I don't have an OBGYN, and I'm not sure how many weeks I am."

She shoved a clipboard stacked with legal forms in my hands. "Fill these out."

Moaning, I passed the clipboard to my mom. "Fill them out for me."

"No, you need to do them yourself. It's for *your* baby," the nurse said.

I rocked side to side on the bed as I attempted to fill out the papers. The pain whipped from my belly to my butthole to my brain, and I began to pray. "Lord, please take the pain away, or take me."

Time tilted as I filled out papers and got my vitals checked, though I remember going about three minutes without any contractions. Then vomit raced up my throat. I barely had a chance to lean my head over the side of the bed. Everything I had eaten the last two days splattered to the hospital floor. Lettuce and bread in whole, and everything else mushed together. I wasn't sure what that meant for my unborn child, but all the doctors came rushing in and pushed me to the delivery room.

"We only have a few minutes to give you an epidural for the pain, but you need to be very still. If you move and the needle hits the wrong spot, you could get paralyzed."

"No. No medication then. I can't… be still." Another contraction started, leaving me too breathless to say more.

"Shh, it's okay. Just be still." My mom held my hand and

brushed my sweaty hair off my forehead. "Trust me, you want that pain medication. I didn't have it with your brother. It was the worst pain of my life. Don't put yourself through that."

Because of my mother's words, I was able to sit hunched over long enough to get the epidural in my spine. The medicine slid down my spine like warm water, and the world went quiet for a moment. When the pressure came again, it wasn't pain, it was power. I could feel my body working for my baby. After I lay my back against the bed, a heavy pressure went from my belly to my vagina. The nurse and nursing student in the labor room told me not to push because the doctor was on his way.

"I have no control over my body!" The pressure was just coming, and on top of it all, I needed to poop.

But then the doctor came running in to wash his hands and put on gloves. He spread my legs to check my cervix one last time and said, "Get ready to push."

I only pushed four times before the doctor screamed, "It's a girl!"

Tears streamed down my face as I sagged back in the bed. "A girl. Oh, thank you, Lord."

The nurses rushed her to the side of the room. Mom stood by my side, still holding my hand. Everything quieted.

Quiet.

Babies weren't quiet.

In the movies, they cried the second they came out. The silence stretched too long. I couldn't breathe. My hands clenched the sheets as I waited for proof that my baby was okay.

The doctors cleaned her face, then spanked her butt twice, and she let off a small whine. It was the most beautiful sound I'd ever heard. Proof that both of us had made it.

Later, they told me that they had to make sure she didn't eat her poop because she was pooping while I was in labor. That was why I vomited.

Her mouth made a sucking motion, so the nurse placed her on my breast to eat. When my baby's warm skin touched mine, my nerves instantly calmed. I counted her tiny toes and fingers and noted that she had two ears, two eyes, and one mouth. Staring at my daughter, I silently prayed to God that my baby was healthy despite my lack of prenatal care. I had never witnessed a human so beautiful. She was milky brown with a dark chocolate left ear. Her curly black hair stuck to her forehead. Her smell was a sweet, relaxing aroma that I had never experienced before.

For the first time in my life, I felt needed in a way that didn't hurt. Every broken part of me began to mend when she blinked up at me.

It was 2:24 a.m. when I gave birth, and shortly after, I went to my recovery room alone as my mom went home. The room felt too big without my mother's voice. The hum of machines became my lullaby. Every cry from the nursery down the hall reminded me that I wasn't just a patient, I was a mother now. Every two hours, the nurse would come and wake me to feed my daughter and check her vitals.

Day two in the hospital, the bliss wore off. Every sound she made startled me. Every cry felt like a question I didn't know how to answer. I checked her diapers to make sure she was dry, I fed her, so I knew she wasn't hungry, and I rocked her, but she continued to cry. And cry. And cry.

Thank God the nurse came in and offered to take her to the nursing station so I could rest. I needed that hour to myself to cry about my situation. With the stitches in my vagina and now a headache because my daughter would not stop crying, I was still in a lot of pain. Everything hurt—my body, my mind, my pride. How was I going to be a good mother when I couldn't even make my own baby stop crying?

The guilt hit just as hard as the fear, and for a moment, I wondered if everyone had been right to doubt me. But then they brought her back, and when her eyes met mine once more, something inside me softened. I remembered my promise to give her the love I'd always wanted. Even through the exhaustion and panic and the questions I didn't know how to answer, that promise felt like the only steady thing I had to hold on to. I entered the hospital as a girl, but I left as a mom—raw, scared, healing, and somehow, stronger than I'd ever been before.

Once home, I set my phone alarm to wake up every two hours for feeding. It seemed like as soon as I fell asleep, the alarm was ringing for me to wake up to feed, and exhaustion set in. Bath time was my favorite because the warm water and bubbles made Tele smirk. It wasn't the big things that made me feel like a mother; it was the tiny ones. The way she gripped my finger when I washed her hair. The way her lips puckered when she dreamed. Though I knew I was in for some trouble because seven days had passed and Tele still refused to suck a pacifier or drink out of a baby bottle.

But my daughter was healthy, and I had enough clothes and

diapers, so I lived in the present. Within a month, I had breastfeeding, diaper changing, tummy time, mother and daughter talk time, and bath time down pat. I felt numb the first year of my daughter's life, like I was moving through an out-of-body experience I couldn't fully wake up from. I still didn't understand how I had become a mother so fast, or how my life had shifted into this new reality where every decision had to be made with someone else in mind. I was young — too young to be carrying that much responsibility — and the exhaustion was constant.

I'd wake up tired, go to school tired, come home tired, and still have to pour whatever energy I had left into caring for her. And underneath all of that was the fear — the quiet, heavy kind that sits in your chest. I didn't know how I was going to provide for my daughter once all the gifts from our families ran out. Every little thing she needed felt like another reminder that I didn't have the resources or the stability I wished I had. I was doing everything I could, but the weight of it all made me feel distant from myself, like I was watching my own life happen from somewhere far away. But I pushed through it all because Tele needed me to.

Tony was happy to have a daughter. He came to visit her at least five times a week. He would hold her in the palm of his right hand and rub her head in a circle with his left hand, saying we had to shape her head. I would just stare at the two of them because Tele would start babbling and Tony would talk, and it seemed that they were having a full conversation. Tele added a new light to Tony's life, so I never revealed to him all the uncertainty I felt in motherhood. I just told myself that it would all work out.

One night, as I watched her sleep, I realized the girl I had been was gone. In her place was someone stronger, quieter, and braver. The pain that once felt unbearable had become the doorway to my purpose.

Reflection: The pain of birth faded when love cried out in my arms — and a new me answered. At that moment, everything I'd endured felt like it was shaping me for this one purpose: to rise, to protect, and to love someone more than I ever thought I could. It was the kind of change that didn't happen gradually, but all at once, settling into my spirit like truth.

Writing Prompt: Write about a time pain turned into purpose, when what once hurt you became the very thing that pushed you to grow.

Broken Success

Chapter 6
Young Motherhood

Once I delivered my baby, the school counselor took me shopping for baby necessities like diapers, wipes, bottles, etc. This was a part of the outreach program Dean Brown set me up with. The school wanted to talk about teen pregnancy prevention and asked if I could give any tips on how the school could make teens more comfortable talking to staff about sex education. When I returned to school after giving birth, they removed me from PE because they felt my body should be healing. Walking down that hallway, my bookbag felt heavier than ever. I wasn't just carrying notebooks anymore; I was carrying responsibility. Every step reminded me that my baby was at home waiting for me to come back with something more than good grades.

Because I was breastfeeding, I kept extra shirts with me. Sometimes the milk would leak out when my breasts were too full. The boys in my class would point at the wet stains on my shirt. "What is that?"

"It's milk because I'm breastfeeding."

"You have a *baby*?"

The boys laughed like it was a joke, like my life was something to point at and whisper about in the hallway. Their comments stung in a way I wasn't prepared for—sharp little reminders that some people only saw the stereotype, not the girl trying to survive inside it. But the girls became my tribe. They didn't see a mistake. They saw a mother trying. They'd text me homework answers, bring baby clothes in their backpacks, and remind me that I was still capable of greatness. Because I didn't have a steady babysitter at the time, I attended school when I could, and my girls brought me classwork on the days I was absent.

That last semester, I struggled with balancing school as a new mom. I could no longer fall into a deep sleep. Instead, I always had an ear open in case my daughter woke up.

Since I had grown up feeling like a burden, I did not want help with my daughter. I would do all my tasks with my daughter at my hip, including taking a shower with her. I would drag myself from class to class on the days that Tony or his family would babysit, but mentally, I could not focus. I was too concerned about what my baby was doing. My mom and brothers would offer to babysit, but I often rejected them. Being the lone wolf and taking care of my daughter alone felt safer. My hard work paid off, and I graduated to high school. The load was heavy, but I was determined that my baby would have a better life than I had.

Each day I prayed. "Father God, please keep my daughter safe physically and mentally. Lord, please keep her after your own heart. Lord, please allow me to provide a stable living environment for her. Lord, please bless me with the tools to love her according to the way she receives love. Amen."

When I whispered "Amen," something lifted. The weight was still there, but it no longer crushed me. At night, I rocked my daughter to sleep and realized I wasn't just carrying her, I was carrying purpose.

In July of 2006, I placed my daughter on the mat for tummy time and sat across the room eating some fried chicken. She mumbled for me to come over to her, but I told her no because I didn't want her fighting me for my chicken. I turned my head toward the TV for about ten seconds, then turned back. She was closer to me. I brushed it off and turned my head back to the TV. Moments later, when I turned back toward her, she was off the mat and only about a foot away from me and my fried chicken.

To ensure my mind wasn't playing tricks on me, I moved to the other side of the room with the chicken plate and watched her crawl to me. I put the plate down and lifted her into my hands, hugging her close and kissing her chubby cheeks. "Tele! Look at you go! Mama is so proud of you."

I was shocked that my daughter was crawling at four months old, yet proud of my baby's motor skills.

The newborn stage was the best for me as a parent. There was something pure and simple about those first months, just her tiny breaths, her warm body curled against mine, and the quiet moments when it felt like the whole world had paused for us. Even with the sleepless nights and constant feedings, that stage felt like a safe place, a time when love was louder than fear, and all she needed was to be held.

The hardest part about the newborn stage was my daughter's ear infections. She would scream at the top of her lungs as she pulled on her ear. After four ear infections in a two-month span, I learned that the ear infections were due to her lying down to breastfeed. So I started sitting up in the middle of the night, holding her upright even when my arms felt weak and my eyes were burning. That small adjustment took patience I didn't know I had and taught me that sometimes the solution comes from paying attention to the little things.

One day, the daycare called me from class because Tele had diarrhea and a fever of 102. Her pediatrician was out of town, so my mom took us to the local emergency room. The doctors ran a lot of tests and told us it was just a stomach virus. "Take her home and give her fluid every two hours to flush out the virus."

"I'm nervous about the fever. I want my daughter to be admitted to the hospital."

"There's nothing the hospital can do that you can't do at home."

Reluctantly, I took Tele home and did what the discharge paper instructed. I spent the next 48 hours filling Tele with fluids and changing her diaper and clothes every 45 minutes because the diarrhea would leak out of the diaper on her clothes and the bedding. In between the fever medication, I rubbed her body down with vinegar to help manage the fever, a remedy my mom taught me. In those 48 hours, I did not eat, sleep, or bathe. My only goal was to get my daughter better. Those two days taught me more about motherhood than any book ever could. I learned to trust my instincts even when they were shaking, to ask for help when I was overwhelmed, and to let the people who loved me step in when I finally couldn't keep going.

Once the virus had passed, Tele bounced back to her cheerful self, and my brothers, my mom, and Tony took turns tending to her while I rested—proof that even when I felt like I was carrying everything alone, I didn't have to. Looking back, that chapter of her ear infections and fevers showed me what real patience looked like, what careful planning required, and how much strength there is in trusting both myself and the people willing to support me. It was chaotic, exhausting, and terrifying, but it shaped me into the kind of mother I promised her I'd be.

All my focus went to school and my baby. There wasn't room for anything else, not my own dreams, not my friendships, not even the pieces of myself that used to make me feel whole. Every day felt like a cycle of responsibility: wake up, take care of the baby, rush to school, come home to take care of the baby, start all over again. I stopped thinking about what I liked or who I wanted to become, because survival came first. It was like the girl I used to be had been packed away somewhere, waiting for a time when I finally had the energy and space to look for her again. But it was worth it. I loved that child with everything in me, and I was determined to give her the best life I possibly could

I wasn't old enough to work, so Tony provided all her finances. My responsibilities were to manage doctor appointments, feed, and entertain her. Life was great. I was accepted into a special school for teen moms and their babies, a place that finally felt like it understood the kind of life I was juggling. Every night, I planned ahead because mornings could fall apart fast. I would lay out our clothes, pack our bags, and line everything up so we could move smoothly before the sun even came up. Planning wasn't optional; it was survival.

We rode the school bus together, her tiny body resting against mine, and throughout the day, I would slip out of class to breastfeed her, then hurry back and try not to fall behind. In my parenting class, I learned how to care for her mental, physical, and emotional health, and each lesson made me feel a little more capable, a little more prepared. It wasn't just about being intentional, thinking ahead, and building the kind of stability I wished someone had built for me. Every routine, every packed bag, every moment I stayed one step ahead was another piece of the mother I was becoming — proof that planning wasn't just a skill, but a lifeline that helped me give her the security I never wanted her to go without.

That school allowed me to face the truth that I'd lost myself in motherhood. As a teenage mom, everything in my life revolved around my daughter — her needs, her schedule, her survival. I didn't have space to think about who I was anymore. The girl I used to be slipped into the background, replaced by someone who was always trying to keep up. But little by little, I started finding pieces of myself again. I began to gain some of myself back as I participated in the drama club and photography classes. I started to feel happy and safe again. This season taught me patience, planning, asking for help, and trusting my instincts.

Reflection: Motherhood demanded everything from me and somehow gave me more than I knew I had.

Writing Prompt: Describe a time responsibility forced you to grow up fast.

Broken Success

Chapter 7
Sisterhood

In the summer of 2006, my older brother turned sixteen and got hired at a local restaurant. With his income, my mom's income, and my child support from Tony, we were able to get an apartment and finally move out of the hotel. I sold snacks and drinks and braided hair at the apartment to help with household necessities.

But two years later, my mom called my two brothers and me to her room. "Y'all need to find other places to live. I can't afford to take care of y'all anymore."

"I'll reach out to my counselor tomorrow," I said. My alternative school had a shelter department that could house my daughter and me.

And that's what I did. But this was just another tactic my mom used to separate herself from me—she and my brothers remained in the apartment together for several months. My mom would stop by to visit Tele and me from time to time, and for my birthday that year, she bought me my first Coach designer bag. I smiled and accepted it, all the while trying to understand how she could afford expensive gifts after saying she could not make ends meet just a few months prior.

Still, the shelter turned out to be a place where I would learn clarity. The rooms were structured like a college dorm with side A and side B, but with a full shared bathroom in the middle, and I shared it with another teen mom and her daughter. On my side was a twin bed for me and a toddler bed for my daughter. We had two tall chests for our clothes and other belongings. Our room always smelled fruity because we were two young girls who sprayed perfume all day. In the kitchen, each mother had assigned cabinets with locks for nonperishable items, along with two shelves in the refrigerator for perishables. We had set curfews for bedtime, when we had to turn our cellphones over to the house mother. Chores for cleaning the common areas were assigned weekly.

But the best part about living in the shelter was the sisterhood — something I didn't even know I was starving for until I finally had it. For the first time in a long time, I wasn't the "teen mom" being whispered about or judged. I was simply one of many girls trying to survive, trying to grow up while raising a tiny human, trying to make the best out of the hand we'd been dealt. Being surrounded by young mothers who shared my reality felt like stepping into a warm room after standing outside in the cold. These girls understood the exhaustion, the fears, the late-night feedings, the guilt, the hope — all without me having to say a word. I learned so much from them, including a ton of cooking recipes, but my favorite was the Rotel dip with red bag

Doritos. Quick, warm in the belly, and full of sweet-and-savory goodness. It tasted like comfort, like girlhood stitched back together.

The other mothers had talents we all depended on: a room down the hall held the girl who braided hair like a professional, and across from me was the artist who put outfits together and wrote our names in fancy lettering for our doors. Our children grew up like cousins, always tumbling around together, and we took turns babysitting so each of us could breathe for a moment. Living at the shelter provided my first experience with therapy. The first time I opened up about how much I still missed my father.

"I miss my father. I miss the girl I was when he was alive. I wish my daughter could have experienced his love."

And I spoke about the lack of love I felt from my mother. How she would always tell me she wanted to abort me because she had just had my older brother seventeen months prior. How the year I was born was the worst year of her life. I spoke of the years she made me feel used as I carried her responsibility for raising my younger brother. I spoke about my fears of motherhood and how often I prayed that I would never make my daughter feel the way my mom made me feel over the years. In therapy, I learned that I had not experienced love the way I needed to. Because of my mom's actions and my dad's death, I built a wall around my heart and told myself I didn't need love. Instead, I focused my energy toward my pockets. If I had money, I would have stability, and I would not put my daughter in a position to be homeless.

Nightly, I would rehearse the Serenity Prayer: "God, please

give me the strength to accept the things I can not change, courage to change the things that I can, and wisdom to know the difference." Each day, I did an activity with my daughter that I wished my mom had done with me, like eating dinner together and baking cookies. I took her on walks to the park and taught her how to ride a bike. Before the shelter, love meant survival. After the shelter, love also meant structure. Before the shelter, love was silent. After the shelter, love meant laughter. Before the shelter, love was expressed as money and gifts. After the shelter, love was expressed in communication and forgiveness.

Reflection: Love wasn't handed to me. I learned to build it, label it, and guard it.

Writing Prompt: Write about a time you created love where it was missing.

Broken Success

Chapter 8
Sweet 16

Late-night shots in the dark. Tony was dead, leaving me 100% responsible for Tele just when I thought my life was getting better.

In 2008, I found my rhythm as a teenage parent. My daughter was up to date with all her shots, she was walking and talking more than the average two-year-old, and my baby girl was potty trained.

Student life was on the ups—I was scheduled to graduate one year early after being told I should consider getting my GED during pregnancy. Taking Florida Virtual online courses laid the foundation for this achievement. I had reached my two-year limit at the alternative school for young mothers and their children, and I was about to step foot into my first traditional high school. I had always been an "A" student because school was the one thing I could control. It was based on my abilities, and only I could let me down. My outgoing personality helped me locate my crowd, and I was good.

When the phone first rang, a little rush of excitement ran

through me. I thought she was calling to say she could babysit, that maybe I'd get a rare weekend to breathe. "Hello, Rachel."

It was Tony's aunt. I assumed she was calling to tell me that she was on her way to pick up Tele at Tony's request, as he had told me the night before.

"Hey, how are you doing?"

The moment she spoke, the air around me shifted. Her voice didn't sound like itself. Something in her tone made my stomach drop before I even understood why.

"Good, and you?"

Then the words came, heavy and shaking, and suddenly, it felt like the world turned beneath me. "Not so good. I'm sorry to have to tell you. Tony got shot early this morning."

"What?" I became dizzy, my heartbeat loud in my ears.

"He died."

"Stop playing."

"You know I would not play like that."

I could hear her talking, but her voice faded in and out, muffled and distant, like she was speaking underwater. My mind tried to catch up, to make sense of what she was saying, but all I could feel was the ground giving way beneath my feet. "I gotta go pick up Tele."

As I walked, I pictured Tony strolling in the door with his 5950 hat on. Tele would grab it from his head and run down the hallway. Sometimes, she would sit in the car on her daddy's lap and turn the steering wheel, thinking she was actually driving. And I know she would miss their playdates at Chick-fil-A, where Tony would make cow noises and feed Tele chicken nuggets and vanilla ice cream. All those moments brought a big smile to my daughter's face, but soon, that smile would fade. I had to tell her that her daddy was dead.

I walked the next few blocks thinking about how I met Tony in a gas station four years prior. He was my type: tall, dark, and handsome with a low-fade haircut. I could see from the corner of my eye that he was staring me down, so I played shy by avoiding eye contact. I asked the cashier about the price of an item, but Tony said, "Get whatever you want. It's on me."

I got everything I wanted, gave Tony a nice smile and a soft thank you, and left. I had yearned for that attention and financial help. My whole life, I was the giver. It felt so good to be on the receiving end for once.

Days later, I saw him at the same store, but that time, he gave me flowers and his phone number. Of course, I didn't call him right away. My gut told me he was a player—his smooth behavior reminded me of my father—but I was new to the city and needed someone to talk with, to laugh with, and Tony became that person. Over the next few years, I cruised the streets with him. He was my tour guide, and he taught me all the Florida lingo, such as jit (person younger than you) and city punch (faucet water), just to name a few. I learned how to distinguish the Haitian, Jamaican, and Hispanic cultures. His knowledge and confidence swaddled me like a newborn's blanket, flaming my desire for him. Before long, our flesh became one, and we created life together. But, in the summer of 2008, the chapter of me, Tony, and the family we planned to create closed.

I flashed back to the night I listened to my mom learn of my father's murder when I was twelve. That cold February night in my grandfather's trailer had been my first experience with death. My stomach muscles had clenched so tight they hurt. I wanted the tears to flow. I wanted to scream. I wanted to beg Tony to come back, but my heart knew it was over. I did all of that when my father died, and it hadn't worked. My father never came back. How could this devastation find me again?

And what made matters worse, I could not be the grieving daughter. This time, I had to be the strong mother. For my dad's homegoing, my clothing and transportation were laid out for me, but for Tony's, I had to shop for our outfits and get us to and from the funeral home. At my dad's funeral, my mom carried me past the casket, and I blacked out both times. At Tony's funeral, I had to weather Tele pushing and screaming as she attempted to get in the casket. My Tele was only two, not old enough to understand death, so the best I could come up with was to tell her that Daddy was in a deep sleep. The selfish part of me wanted her to stay right there with me. She was my strength and the only one who provided me with the purpose I needed to push past my grief.

Unfamiliar faces packed the muggy room, filled with the smells of so many undesirable things, but I found comfort in being in the room with him one last time. Losing both men to gun violence brought confusion and questions into my life. *Why do people feel they have the right to kill another person? Why is this curse following me? Does the reason he's no longer here have something to do with me?* Mentally, I was a mess. I feared Tele would end up just like me, looking for love in all the wrong places because her father was not there to protect her anymore. Grief is such a manipulator!

First, my daddy, and now, my daughter's daddy. How much more pain would I have to take?

After the homegoing, I had to create new routines for my daughter and me. It was my responsibility to reassure my daughter that she was still safe without her father. That she was still smart and powerful without her father. It was now my responsibility to raise my daughter to feel fulfilled rather than missing a parent. I gave her a picture of the two of them together, and before bedtime, she would give him a good-night kiss.

I took motherhood more seriously after Tony's death. All our finances were on me, so I got a job. For the next year, I went to school Monday–Friday and worked Friday–Sunday. When I wasn't at school or work, I took my daughter to as many outings as I could. I had no time to focus on normal sixteen-year-old issues like after-school sports, dating, or parties. My focus was on monthly budgeting skills and how to grow credit. In my senior year, I skipped prom, one of the most memorable nights, because I didn't want to mess up my budget. It broke my heart because I had always looked forward to prom. I daydreamed about wearing a long glittery Cinderella dress, wearing my hair in a half-up, half-down curly weave updo, and arriving in a nice limo with my friends. Nobody could have stolen my joy that night.

Prom would stay a dream, but my goals would become reality. My goal was to graduate from high school and go to college to become a schoolteacher—a career that allowed me to be hands-on with my daughter. In May 2009, I walked the stage and officially became a high school graduate. It wasn't just a ceremony for me. It was a mountain I had climbed with a baby on my hip, grief on my back, and a future I refused to give up on pulling me forward.

My emotions were everywhere at once. I was proud, deeply proud, that my daughter got to see me cross that stage, proof that I was fighting for our life every single day. But that pride came tangled with sadness that felt just as heavy. My angels weren't there. I kept imagining my father in the crowd, smiling that proud smile of his, finally softening enough to let me get those artificial nails he swore he'd never allow. And I knew in my heart Tony would've thrown me the biggest graduation party anyone had ever seen. That's the family that I should've had. That's the family that should've been cheering. But that wasn't the hand I was dealt.

Instead, I paid for everything myself. And stood in my own strength because neither my father nor Tony were there to witness what I had fought so hard to achieve. And in true Shawntae fashion, I didn't show a single crack. I didn't mention their names or let anyone see the ache sitting in my chest. I smiled for the pictures, held my diploma tight, and pretended the victory didn't hurt. But inside, I was both triumphant and broken—walking that stage not just as a graduate, but as a survivor of everything that tried to stop me from getting there.

Reflection: My Sweet 16 was draped in black, yet I still found light. Even in grief, God kept placing small lanterns along my path—my daughter's laughter, my graduation day, my own resilience. Light was still there; I just had to lift my head high enough to see it.

Writing Prompt: Write about a time when life felt overwhelmingly dark, yet small moments of light helped guide you forward — moments that reminded you that you were stronger, more supported, or more resilient than you realized.

Shawntae Bennett

Broken Success

Chapter 9
Rising Higher

Life had finally started moving forward, but my heart was still catching up. I was balancing motherhood, survival, and the weight of being so close to adulthood yet still dependent on people I didn't always feel safe with. Graduating from high school began a new chapter for my daughter and me. But I was only seventeen, so I still needed my mom's permission for legal stuff.

    I enrolled in college at night so my daughter could stay in our room and sleep under my mom's and my brothers' care. Work promoted me to shift manager, which came with a dollar pay raise that I desperately needed, though it still wasn't enough. The school board no longer paid for daycare since I had finished school, and the government daycare assistance program waitlist was extensive. I hated dragging my daughter to work with me, but I had no other choice. I worked at a restaurant in the food court, so I sat her at a table in front so I could watch her and work. My daughter said that it was fun because she got to eat at different places in the food court. Others knew she was my daughter and would bring her toys and spend their lunch break with her. But while she saw it as an adventure, I lived each shift with a knot in my stomach, praying no one judged me as a bad mother, praying no one called the police on me, praying she stayed safe while I hustled to survive.

Sure enough, an older customer got upset with my supervisor for allowing me to work while my baby sat in the food court. I explained, "I don't have childcare, and without this job, me and my baby would be homeless."

She softened then, understanding the situation. "Call 211. It's an information line to different resources in the area."

I called, and they got me in touch with a daycare that offered a sliding scale to help families in need. Relief washed over me that following Monday as I walked my daughter into a real daycare. A weight lifted off my chest. I could finally breathe again. I could focus on work, knowing she would be cared for, watched, played with, and treated like the child she was, not a quiet shadow waiting for her mama. It filled me with happiness I hadn't felt in a long time. But at that point, my older brother moved back to South Carolina, so without his income, we had to move back to a hotel. My daughter was older this time around, so I didn't want her cramped up in one room with me, my mom, and my younger brother. I wanted her to have space to run around. Not to mention, that hotel was known for drug trafficking, prostitution, and many other illegal activities. I wanted her to be safe when she walked outside our home.

Inside the room, things were the same as they had always been. My mom complained about everything I did or didn't do, every complaint a reminder that I was still a child in her eyes, even though I was raising one of my own. I swallowed my hurt because I needed a roof over our heads, but the silence between us grew louder every day.

The day before I turned eighteen, my mom convinced the hotel manager to give me my own room, so my daughter and I moved to the other side of the building. All I wanted for my birthday was a safe place to live. I didn't expect anything to change, but that small act became the push I needed. It reminded me that even in chaos, God always slipped in small mercies to keep me going. Within a week, we moved into our first apartment in downtown Orlando. That older apartment didn't have central heat or air, and I would later learn of the roach infestation, but Tele and I learned to enjoy our new place. It was a one-bedroom, one-bath, and we had zero furniture, so we slept on an air mattress, but it was ours. We swam in the complex pool on days I didn't have to work. There were more kids in the complex, so my daughter could play with children her own age.

Still, my daughter was getting older, and the bills were increasing. I needed to find a way to lessen my work and go to college more. Graduating from college meant earning more money, which would give me the freedom to be present in my daughter's life. That break would come when I got approved for the government housing projects in my city. I was excited by how well-kept the apartment was compared to my last one. No more roaches, and we had central heat and air. And Tony's family ensured our apartment got fully furnished.

The Griffin Park Apartments felt like the Bayside Manor Apartments I had lived in long ago. Kids knocked on the door, asking if Tele could come play. Neighbors shared rides, meals, and motherly advice. For the first time, I didn't feel like a visitor in my own life. I felt rooted in a place where everyone looked out for one another. A place to grow long-lasting friendships, as the kids fought one day and were friends the next. Our apartment was right next to the park and basketball court, so I could watch Tele play from our kitchen window as I cooked dinner. Most importantly, what I used to pay in rent at my old apartment covered my rent and utilities in my government apartment.

With a safe, stable place to live, I could focus on getting a vehicle. I saved for months, and then tax time came around, so I used all that money to buy a gold 1998 Nissan Maxima. We named her Pocahontas. For the first time, I felt like I truly deserved to be a mother, not because I was perfect, but because I had built something from nothing. My daughter was housed, fed, and clothed, yes, but more than that. She was nurtured, guided, and surrounded by love. In our little place, with our routines and our laughter and our lessons, I realized I hadn't just created a home for her. I had finally created one for myself too.

Reflection: Rising higher meant carrying my daughter with me through every milestone. Rising higher wasn't about escaping my past; it was about rewriting the future in real time, with my daughter watching me climb.

Writing Prompt: Write about a time you proved people wrong by achieving more than expected.

Chapter 10

Healing the Girl, Guiding the Mother

Shawntae, because you got pregnant, your life is over. Many young women hear this when they become pregnant out of wedlock, but when you're a baby having a baby, you get a double dose of it. Society sees you as fast, as hot in the pants, and somehow, you taught yourself how to be.

Please understand, I was taught sex. I recall a time when my older brother, my mom, and I were sitting in the apartment. A popular rap song came on, and the artist made a comment about making an object disappear only using her mouth. I said, "I'd like to learn that," like she was a magician teaching magic tricks.

Then it was my favorite female rapper, a sexual icon who used her gritty words and pretty face as tools to persuade men to give her whatever she wanted. And there I was again, in my mother's and older brother's presence, reciting the lyrics of her music, saying, "That is the kind of woman I am going to be."

My mom shook her head. "That's not good." But she didn't explain why I should not want to be like these women, nor did she explain the type of woman I should strive to be. She didn't explain that the songs were about sex and how sex was created by God for married couples to reproduce.

As an adult, when I listen to the same music that I grew up on, my mind is blown by the words coming out of the artist's mouth. This was the music that raised me and the examples displayed in something I viewed as art, and they were the examples I followed. But no one informed me that sometimes music is figurative, not literal.

Then there were the movies with the elaborate sex scenes, and yes, I was told to close my eyes, and indeed I did, but my ears were still open. I remember one movie where the woman was in an abusive relationship, and in one scene, the husband raped her. I closed my eyes, but their moans and groans, one of pleasure and one of pain, sent shocks through my virgin vagina. And all I could remember was wanting to feel those shock waves again.

It started as me being the lookout for my older brother and cousins when they snuck company into their bedrooms. Afterward, I would listen to the stories of their enjoyment. And before long, I found an older boy in my neighborhood who was willing to take the chance of sneaking into my bedroom. Through music, movies, and now experience, I had become promiscuous.

When I finally acted on my curiosity, it gave me a newfound power. I was in control. I was feeling myself, and nobody could tell me anything! There was a rush in knowing I had stepped into a world I had only wondered about, a world that felt grown and dangerous and thrilling all at once. Carrying that secret made me feel untouchable. It was like I had this hidden confidence tucked under my clothes, something that belonged only to me. And even though I didn't fully understand what I was chasing, it felt good to have something that made me forget every insecurity, every loss, every reason I had ever felt small.

Living with a single parent with very limited supervision allowed this behavior to travel in every direction that I wanted it to go. At no time did I comprehend that this behavior would lead to pregnancy. Yet it did.

Now, at 32 years old, I will tell you this: Teenage pregnancy saved my life. Being a mother allowed me to slow down, analyze my actions, and research my environment, not just recite and perform the things I heard and saw.

I didn't become a responsible teen mother overnight; I had help from a very special mentor—Mrs. Brandy. She had the power to see beyond my smile and made me feel comfortable. With a calm honesty, she explained what things were not my fault versus the actions I needed to take accountability for. She stressed the importance of finding my voice so I could always speak up for myself. Refusing to accept the bare minimum from me, she pushed in ways no one else had, asking me the kind of probing questions that challenged me to dig deeper. And she gave me parenting books and strategies to help me develop a parenting style. Because of all that, I gained confidence and felt truly seen by her. Mrs. Brandy would end our sessions by setting attainable goals for the next session.

Once my daughter was at the mimicking stage, I stopped

listening to the dirty Southern street music that I grew up on. No more popular movies or TV shows. I stopped ignoring the warning labels on movies and music to ensure she interacted with age-appropriate content. I even stayed away from the social media wave that was on the rise. When Tele brought home topics from the school or the playground, I clarified all the language. And I kept her away from people who exhibited adult behaviors or had adult conversations around kids. Nature, gospel, and game shows were our life.

Inappropriate content still reached her though. One of her older cousins introduced Tele to a dancing app. She came home from a weekend with her cousin, performing an adult song from the app. I sat her down and explained, "Your movements and words are not age-appropriate. Don't do either of them again."

Days later, my daughter ignored my instructions and performed to the adult song again. This time, I grabbed a belt and applied pain to her backside as I repeated my previous words. That situation was the foundation for my daughter's interaction with the outside world. To this day, if that adult song comes on, my daughter reminds me of the time I laid down the law about what was acceptable in our household.

Teaching her all the things I was never taught brought up feelings I didn't expect. There were moments when I'd look at her and think about how different my life might have been if someone had taught me about boundaries, intuition, and real love before the world tried to teach me the hard way. Sometimes it hurt, knowing I had to learn through pain what she got to learn through guidance. But even in that ache, I understood something deeper: if my mother had taught me everything I needed to know back then, I might not have stumbled the way I did, but stumbling is what led me to Tele. As much as I wish I'd been spared certain heartbreaks, I wouldn't trade them, because every mistake, every struggle, every tear is what brought this beautiful child into my life. And teaching her felt like rewriting my own past — healing the younger me while protecting the girl I was raising.

A few months ago, I had the pleasure of meeting a young mother I will call Kayla. She stood in the store aisle with her cart half-filled, trying to focus on the list in her hand while her son cried so hard his little body shook. Even from across the aisle, I recognized the look on her face — the tight jaw, the trembling breath, the way she blinked fast to keep the tears from spilling over. I could almost feel her frustration, that mix of exhaustion and helplessness that only a mother in the thick of it truly understands. Her eyes glossed over as she tried to soothe him and shop at the same time, and at that moment, she reminded me of myself all those years ago. So I did what the nurse had done for me when I thought I was drowning. I walked over and offered Kayla some help.

"Hi, I'm Shawntae. I've been where you are right now, and I would love to help. Why don't you sit and tend to your son while I get everything on your list? Or would you rather I hold him while you focus on shopping?"

A tear from each eye fell down her cheeks as she handed me her son. "Thank you, Jesus," she whispered. "His name is Kaleb. He's got a stomach virus."

I walked the store with mom and son, helping her pick out the best items to help during his sickness and sharing some home remedies my mom had taught me. Once we finished shopping, I could tell Kayla had received the mental break she needed to regroup. I was thankful too—grateful that I could be there for Kayla and Kaleb in a moment that could have easily broken her spirit. As I walked away, memories of my worst encounters with people flashed through my mind. They would see me struggling with my daughter, and instead of offering help, they would ask me how old I was. All the times I would be telling a happy memory about my daughter, they would respond with, "Oh my, you don't look old enough to have a daughter that age." Their words were never concern, just judgment disguised as curiosity. And in those moments, I always wished someone had stepped toward me with compassion instead of stepping back in criticism.

I became the guiding light I once searched for. Every lesson I taught my daughter, every young mother I support, every moment I choose tenderness over judgment—these are the ways I rewrite my own story. I couldn't control the guidance I never received, but I can control the guidance I give. And in choosing to be what I needed, I didn't just raise my daughter, I'm healing the girl I used to be and illuminating the path for the women coming behind me.

Reflection: I learned about sex from songs and screens that glorified the very things that wounded me, but motherhood taught me a different language—one rooted in honesty, intuition, and protection. Teaching my daughter the lessons I never had felt like rewriting the script that shaped me. And each time I reach back to help another mother, I'm healing a piece of the girl I once was. Breaking cycles isn't loud or easy; sometimes it's as simple as choosing to be the woman I needed.

Writing Prompt: Write about a time you chose to give someone the guidance, love, or protection you once wished someone had given you. What cycle were you trying to break, and how did it change you?

Chapter 11

Raising a Teen

No one warns you that raising a teenager feels like raising a mirror, one that reflects your fears, your wounds, and your deepest hopes all at once.

One Tuesday afternoon, I was walking into a local middle school to register my daughter for the upcoming school year. My daughter had been accepted into a magnet school that placed emphasis on the arts. Tele's specialty was dance, so she was excited to learn more styles of dance. My baby girl was heading into sixth grade, and that thought alone made my stomach twist. Would she leave middle school pregnant, like I did?

At the time, Tele hadn't gotten her period yet, which gave me a small sense of relief, but the fear didn't disappear. For months, I worried about peer pressure. Her old school was full of families like ours, working-class, doing their best with what they had. No one questioned her background because most of the kids shared the same struggles. But this new school was different. Most students came from upper-class, two-parent households, with resources I could never compete with. I worried she might feel out of place or, worse, be influenced in ways I couldn't predict. Before her first day, I sat her down and explained my heart plainly: that this school wasn't just a change of scenery, but an opportunity. I told her I hoped she'd use it to strengthen her creativity, explore new horizons, and grow, not get caught up in drama or try to fit into spaces that weren't meant for her spirit.

Then the first sign of her bad attitude arrived. One morning, she asked casually, "Can I have ten dollars? We're going to the coffee shop later." Her middle school was across the street from a coffee shop, so some teachers would walk them over as a mini field trip.

I raised a brow. "For what? You're young. You don't need no coffee."

She rolled her eyes so hard I thought they'd get stuck. "Oh my God, everyone gets something. I'm going look dumb just standing there."

"No, coffee isn't for kids."

She huffed, snatched her backpack, and slammed the door behind her.

Later that day, I spoke with another mother who explained that they don't give the teens caffeine; they just give them a cute little coffee-looking drink that makes them feel cool. I understood then why my daughter gave me lip. It wasn't that she wanted to drink coffee. She didn't want to feel left out. I bought a reloadable gift card for the coffee shop that she could use to make purchases. Case one solved.

Next, Tele brought to my attention that all the kids at her school had cell phones. We had a strict routine, so I didn't understand why she needed a phone. Tele explained, "I need to be part of the dance group chats to stay on top of upcoming performance opportunities."

Hearing her say that made my heart thump in a way I couldn't hide. Terrified that history would repeat itself, I was not okay with getting Tele a cell phone. Having a phone at her age had given me too much freedom, too much privacy — enough quiet corners to make choices I wasn't ready for, choices that shaped my whole life. It's what led to my pregnancy. I wasn't just saying no to a device; I was saying no to the shadow of the girl I used to be, the one who hid behind secrets because she didn't know how to ask for help. The fear that Tele might unknowingly step onto the same path lived in my chest like a ticking clock, each second a reminder of how quickly innocence could shift into responsibility.

I reached out to my older brother about the situation, and he agreed to give Tele an old iPhone he had. We connected the phone using my email so I could monitor what Tele was doing. At first, things were fine. She used it mostly for dance group chats and staying connected with friends. But as the weeks went on, I started to feel her drifting. Not in a dramatic, rebellious way. But in the small, subtle shifts that only a mother notices. Longer in her room, shorter conversations with me, more giggles at a screen than at the things we used to do together. I didn't know if it was the phone, the new school environment, or simply the age she was entering, but it felt like something was pulling her attention away from me inch by inch.

Then the COVID pandemic closed schools for the remainder of the school year. Being home together during COVID molded us back together again. I became more than an ATM machine and a taxicab driver. We went back to cooking together and watching shows. It felt great having my best friend back. We got to reminisce about all her school plays and sporting events. My favorite part of being home was the way she slowly gravitated back into my bed at night, the same little girl who used to curl into me. It felt like we'd found each other again in the middle of a chaotic world.

Tele was thrilled about starting high school, especially knowing she'd been accepted into the nursing program. Her ambition lit something in me too — watching her dream out loud pushed me to start setting new goals for myself, the same way she was bravely shaping her own future. But when August rolled around and she officially entered high school, the excitement didn't last long. By the time the second nine weeks hit, the emails began rolling in, and what I had hoped would be a fresh chapter for her quickly started to feel more like "hell school." Tardy second period, tardy fourth period, tardy sixth period. When she got home, I would ask her, "Why were you tardy to so many different classes?"

"It's impossible to reach certain classes on time. They're too far apart."

I came up with an idea. I told Tele that for every class she was tardy to, I would hold her phone for 24 hours. Magically, Tele was never tardy to class again.

But then the phone calls started about her grade in her nursing class—she was *failing*. I continued encouraging her. "The work is always hard in the beginning, but it will get easier."

Tele wasn't happy, and she asked for months on end to drop out of the nursing program. I refused to allow her to quit. "I did not raise no quiter. You are too young to have a quitting spirit. If you quit now, you're training your brain that every time something gets hard, it's quitting time."

This conflict drove a wedge between her and me, and sometimes we would go days without speaking. Each silent day felt heavier than the last. I could feel her pulling away, her frustration stacking on top of my fears. Part of me worried I was being too hard on her; another part believed I was protecting her future the only way I knew how. But standing my ground came with a cost—I missed her laughter, her random stories, even her teenage eye rolls. It hurt to watch her shut me out, yet it hurt even more to imagine her walking away from something she once believed she could do.

Still, I pushed to make sure she had all the resources she needed to be successful, which included getting her driver's license. One Saturday, I allowed her to take my car to pick something up from a friend down the street. Next thing I knew, hours had passed without her return, so I called her. She answered, and I told her she needed to come home. She agreed. Another couple of hours passed. Still no Tele.

I called my friend for a ride to Tele's friend's house. When I arrived and saw my car, my heart dropped—the entire front left side of the bumper was crushed in. Tele stood there looking guilty, and that's when she told me she'd been in an accident. I was livid. Not just because of the damage, but because she never called me. I kept thinking, *Why wouldn't you reach out? Why wouldn't you tell me?*

It didn't take long for the truth to come out. She hadn't crashed near her friend's house at all. She'd taken my car on a joy ride, detouring where she had no business being, and that's where the accident happened. Finding that out felt like a slap — the secrecy, the recklessness, the complete disregard for the trust I'd placed in her.

So, I revoked her driving privileges, and the distance between us grew even wider. She was angry. I was disappointed. And underneath all of it, I felt a deep sadness, realizing how far we had drifted from the closeness we once shared. Our home became a war zone. Monday through Friday, it was some disagreement pertaining to school: not waking up on time, not dressing appropriately, or skipping English class. On Saturday, it was her lack of effort in cleaning the house. "If you don't like how I do it, you do it."

Then on Sundays, she no longer wanted to go to church. "Not everyone who goes to church is going to heaven."

Everything I said, Tele had something slick to say, and I would punish her by taking her phone. One particular day, she was tired of me taking her phone, so she grabbed a knife from the kitchen and threatened to kill herself. Time froze. My breath left my body, and for a moment, fear swallowed every part of me. I didn't see a rebellious teenager; I saw my baby girl drowning in emotions she didn't have the tools to handle.

I quickly learned that she didn't really intend to harm herself; she just put on a dramatic performance with the hopes of getting her way. And it worked. I felt defeated. I went to my bedroom and hid under the covers and wept. I was at rock bottom. How could this be my sweet baby girl? Where did I go wrong in raising her? She went to stay at her friend's house for a week.

For five days, I gave up. I couldn't carry the weight of being a single mother anymore. I prayed every time I was alone — in the shower at home, or in my car at work, I cried. And then, I began practicing what I had learned from my grand-aunt growing up. She would say, "Open your mouth and tell God what you want."

So, I prayed. "God, make me whole again. Grant me the serenity to accept the things I cannot change, courage to change things that I can, and wisdom to know the difference."

Day six, I felt stronger. With every tear that fell, I would say, "Lord, may the tears I cry in this season water my blessings for the next season."

On day seven, I went to pick my daughter up from her friend's house, who took her in after the incident. The car ride was silent, but when we got in the house, I started up again, telling her how the school was calling about her being absent. I made her clean the house, and she had to be in my sight at all times. I tried to do the mommy and me journal I found in a parenting group, where we would take turns writing to each other instead of talking because Tele would accuse me of yelling. But that didn't work. I wanted Tele to know how she hurt me, and she didn't have that understanding. She came home like we had not been apart for a week. She came home like everything should go back to normal, and that made me angry.

I signed up for family counseling, and after the first session, the therapist told me, "Y'all don't need family counseling. *You* need counseling."

It stung at first, but it was the truth I didn't know I needed. She saw the exhaustion in my eyes before I even opened my mouth. Hearing a professional say I was the one who needed counseling felt like someone gently placing a mirror in my hands and asking me to finally look. It wasn't an attack—it was an invitation. Still, accepting it wasn't easy. There's a unique kind of ache that comes with realizing you might be part of the chaos you've been blaming on someone else.

But buried inside that ache was something powerful: the possibility of healing. Admitting that I needed help didn't make me weak—it made me brave. It meant breaking generational patterns instead of passing them down. It meant choosing growth over pride, clarity over defensiveness, and accountability over denial. I understood that the strongest thing a mother can do is confront the parts of herself that hurt the child she loves. And at that moment, painful as it was, I took my first real steps toward becoming the woman—and mother—I truly wanted to be. Celebrating my daughter's accomplishments was the start of clearing up what I thought went wrong in raising her. First was the nurse pinning ceremony. Tele managed to stay the course and complete the program. Then it was her high school graduation, my proudest mommy moment of her teenage years.

It was an excellent close to a major chapter in our lives.

Baby Tele and Teenage Tele were not the same person. Baby Tele just wanted to be next to her mom, play at the park, and get a vanilla ice cream cone from the store. Teenage Tele wanted designer shoes, a custom prom dress, and to order DoorDash multiple times a day. But Teenage Tele also spoke her true feelings. She was goal-driven and a hard worker. I had been a fragile teen due to my mommy-pleasing issues. The fact that Tele was so strong-minded healed the teenager in me. It amazed me how someone so strong came from someone so broken.

Reflection: Watching my daughter become a young woman was like watching the best parts of myself bloom again, but stronger, freer, and wiser. Raising a teen didn't just stretch me; it softened me. It taught me that love evolves, and so must we.

Writing Prompt: Write about someone you raised, mentored, or guided—and how their growth taught you something about yourself.

Chapter 12

Success

Success never arrives wrapped in confidence. It usually shows up disguised as obstacles, delays, and tests that force you to grow.

"Ms. Bennett, I've looked over your paperwork, and I see that you've received a significant increase in your income. Still, at this time, we can't approve your home loan application. Please reapply in six more months so we can ensure that your new position is permanent."

Something inside me sank at those words. By the time I heard the same words a second time, I couldn't even lift my eyes off the floor. It felt like someone had placed a concrete wall in front of my future. I had done everything "right," yet life still told me, "Not yet." My credit was in the seven hundreds, and I was debt-free, but still, many banks found reason after reason to deny my application.

Even during this trial, I kept the faith by remembering the story of David and Goliath. David was a regular young man, smaller and less experienced than the mighty warrior Goliath, yet David volunteered to fight Goliath to save his people. In the end, little David, with big faith, defeated Goliath. For every success I've had, I started out like David, who everyone thought would suffer defeat. Every battle in my life started with me standing small, unsure, with limited resources, but my faith always gave me aim.

My first round of success came in 2009 when I graduated from high school as a single teen mother. My hard work had finally paid off, and I had given people something positive to say about me. I had endured Tony's death and my father's death, yet I had closed the chapter titled "The Fear of Being a High School Dropout." That accomplishment ignited a fire in me, reminding me that I could overcome any obstacle.

When I entered college, I was David because I had no experience with college life. Neither of my parents had attended college, so I was back in unfamiliar territory, filling out financial documents alone to make sure I received my Pell Grants on time. I would wake up to nightmares of being denied entry. Every day, I second-guessed every decision I made. *What if I'm not smart enough and end up dropping out?*

Math nearly ended my college career. In my first semester, I had to take a remedial math course. I sat in the adviser's office crying for a third opportunity to take college algebra. I explained, "I don't have time to take the course at a different college. I'm only taking one class this semester, and I already created a plan to visit the math center for extra tutoring three times a week."

When I was granted the chance to retake the course a third

time, I felt a surge of hope. I followed my plan with discipline, and finally, I passed. Though doubt overshadowed my joy. How far could I get through college if it took me three semesters to pass college algebra? I pushed that feeling aside, determined not to give up. Every passed quiz felt like a miracle. Every completed assignment reminded me that I wasn't fighting for a degree, I was fighting for a future my daughter could depend on.

My favorite class in college was speech. I have always loved to speak in front of people, and this class allowed me to do just that. While most students were still tired during that seven-a.m. class, I always came ready. I was the first to do my speech the entire semester. Taking the initiative to be first every time made me a favorite among my classmates, though I didn't have time for a college social life. I was still working full-time to pay my bills on top of being a single mother.

On August 3, I officially graduated, a milestone made even sweeter by the fact that it fell on my father's birthday. I decorated my cap, celebrating my dad's birthday—his gift from me. I praised God for allowing me to honor my father in such a special way because my dad did not finish high school. He would have been so proud of me.

And the gifts kept coming. My employer offered me a promotion. I started my first teaching assignment one week after graduation. Standing in front of my classroom, pretending I had it all together, my hands trembled. I carried the weight of three hundred futures. But when the students filed in one by one, something clicked. I wasn't just teaching lessons. I was becoming the stability I never had. Did I have all the skills needed to take my students to the next level?

For 180 days, I gave every ounce of myself to my craft: building relationships, studying the curriculum, and explaining the lessons to my students. My hard work paid off when I was appointed Teacher of the Year Nominee by my coworkers. Their nomination felt like a quiet affirmation that all the late nights, all the studying, and all the heart I poured into that classroom had not gone unseen.

Then I was back to feeling like David when it was time to buy a home. The lenders said that I didn't have enough income to purchase the single-family home I desired. One minute it was the income, then it was the savings amount, then it was the longevity of the income. I nearly changed my mind about being a homeowner. I hated jumping through so many hoops. I didn't have the endurance to keep participating in this home-buying marathon. But just when I was about to change course, I received a phone call from a seller. Within a month's time, I closed on the single-family home I'd prayed for. When the keys finally hit my palm, I just stood there for a moment—breathing, smiling, letting it sink in that this time, life had finally said yes. Now, I had the education, the job, and the house, but something was still missing.

I still felt broken. It was as if I had stacked accomplishment on top of accomplishment, hoping they would fill the empty spaces inside me, only to realize the cracks were still there. Again, I turned to therapy, but this time it was different. My goal was to move past my brokenness and become whole. The process of making a therapy appointment was as simple as making a doctor's appointment. The receptionist didn't respond to me like she thought I was a crazy person, as I had feared. As soon as we hung up the phone, I burst into tears—tears of relief that whispered, "Now you love yourself."

The day of my appointment, the nerves came rushing back. I made sure to arrive early, my heart thumping the whole ride there. The office was tucked inside a multi-purpose building, which oddly eased some of my anxiety—no one passing by would know which door I was walking through or why.

The lobby was calm and simple, painted a soft brown with two orange sofas facing a wooden coffee table scattered with a few magazines. After checking in, I was escorted down a quiet hallway into the therapy room. The walls were a gentle light blue, decorated with pictures of dolphins gliding through waves. I took a seat on the dark blue couch across from my therapist, and terror crawled up my spine.

I was scared to let her see the real me.

What if she thought I was unstable and needed to be admitted somewhere?

What if she thought I was dramatic—just a grown woman crying about things other people had survived worse versions of? All my thoughts came to a halt when my therapist asked me in a mellow voice, "How are you doing today?"

Tears spilled down my face before any words came out, and she allowed me to cry. It felt like releasing twenty years of pain in one breath. No judgment. No yelling. Just space, a safe, quiet space, to finally tell the truth. When I calmed, she asked what made me cry.

"No one has asked me that question in years."

She repeated the question, and I summarized my life over the course of an hour. I left with homework to complete before our next session. In future sessions, I broke down my childhood and used it to understand my current habits. I studied my triggers and how they manifested into bad habits, slowly being reborn into the version of me I wanted to be instead of the girl trauma had created. I spent seven weeks in therapy unlearning everything my traumas had taught me.

When I no longer thought of the worst-case scenario every time I met a new person or was presented with a new opportunity, I knew therapy had helped me. Now, I operate with the three circles my therapist taught me about. One is things I have no control over. I push them out of my head immediately. The second circle is things I can control but don't need to be completed right away. For example, how I'll pay next month's light bill. That can wait until next month. Circle number three is what I can control and needs to be handled in the next 24–48 hours, like cooking dinner, doing schoolwork, etc. In this circle, I learned to do first what is due first, and that reduces my anxiety. Therapy helped me take accountability for my future rather than my past because my past failures were not mine to bear—I had been an unguided child.

One day, I found myself sitting at the table with my two brothers and my daughter, reminiscing about our childhood. As we talked, something settled over me—soft at first, then unmistakable. My daughter had never lived the trauma we survived. She had never felt the instability, the fear, the uncertainty that shaped so much of who we became.

At that moment, pride swelled in my chest. I could say, without hesitation, that my daughter had lived with me her entire life. She had known stability, safety, and love — things I once only prayed for. Watching her sit there, free from the burdens that weighed us down, made something clear to me: breaking generational pain isn't just an accomplishment. It is the greatest success of all. Like David, I learned that the real giants weren't the people or problems. It was the belief that I couldn't win. Once I conquered that, every victory became possible. They said I couldn't finish school — but God made a way. They said I couldn't buy a home, but God multiplied what little I had.

Reflection: Success wasn't one moment — it was every step I refused to quit. Every Goliath I faced only revealed a stronger version of David in me.

Writing Prompt: Write about a time success looked different from what you expected.

Shawntae Bennett

Chapter 13

Full Circle

The giant was never the world; it was the belief that I didn't deserve more. Once that giant fell, everything else followed.

I thought my story was about survival, but it was really about turning broken places into beautiful sanctuaries. I realized this in the summer of 2024, the day I was driving to drop my daughter off at college. Three generations cursed to enter parenthood before the age of eighteen had been broken — Tele was the first out of my grandmother, mother, and me to live on a college campus. During the four-hour drive from our home to her dorm, I reminisced about Tele. How she was like her mama, confident in her academics, how she was well-balanced, which I titled an "educated party girl." Still, like me, I could feel her desire for her father. I could see the wonder in her eyes. *What if he was still here? How would my life be different?* I could hear her whispers to God, asking, "Why did you choose me to be fatherless?"

As I continued on Interstate 95 North, I prayed that my Tele would keep perseverance in her life, understanding that every step forward contributed to her overall success. Praying that she remembered that once you worked hard for something, you rest in your results because you did all you could. Praying that she left self-doubt behind because she had enough people underestimating her abilities. She did not need to do it either. Most importantly, I prayed that she leave the what-ifs behind. Her life was exactly how it was supposed to be to fulfill God's purpose.

Hour two, I drifted in my thoughts about how the broken pieces of me were now beautiful. I thought back to being eighteen years old and how excited I was to get my first apartment so Tele and I could move from the drug-infested hotel. Fast forward ten plus years, I was a homeowner. I thought about the times I had to take her to work with me, the times we had to live in the apartment with no electricity because my hours had gotten cut at work, but now, my career offered a salary that allowed me to maintain all the bills.

I thought about the younger me who depended on school lunch for daily meals, the teen mom who depended on the government food stamp program to feed her daughter. Now, I was self-sufficient. During this ride, I realized I was not a baby with a baby anymore. I had grown into a responsible woman who was aware and prepared for the world. I was proud that I became a mother because motherhood taught me how to live, love, and laugh. It taught me how to forgive myself for getting pregnant, detouring the life I had previously planned. Through it all, I finally understood that the end was only death. New beginnings are everything before, because life is a series with different volumes and titles that work together to create a legacy.

Hour three, I thought, *What do I want my legacy to be?* A warm tear dropped from my eye as a picture of my late grandfather flashed in my mind. One year prior to my daughter leaving for college, we said our final goodbyes to my grandfather, Cleveland. Losing him reopened wounds I thought had healed, but it also revealed how deeply I craved truth and guidance, values he lived every day. This was a difficult time for me because he had become a father figure once my father passed away. I sat in the second row at his funeral, listening to every speaker, from classmates to neighbors to siblings, kids, grandkids, and great-grandkids. Though they all used different words, my grandfather's characteristics were the same.

My grandfather was a man of truth, both ugly and beautiful. He was never a person to call rotten ripe, and if one dared to get upset at his observation, he would simply say, "Go somewhere else if you want to be lied to."

This is the legacy I want to leave behind, one of truth, that a person's foundation does not dictate their final destination. I want people to remember all the obstacles that stood in my way and how I tackled them all one by one. I want people to remember how I turned trials into victories with a smile on my face. How I spread peace into every atmosphere I entered. How I inspired those who came behind me to turn every problem into a privilege with the understanding that God equipped them for this very purpose. When I was broken, I would wonder where God was and why He was allowing me to go through all these hardships. In healing, I learned that God is always with me, and it is my responsibility to tap into Him daily because He wants a relationship with me. If I only acknowledge Him in bad times, that will increase my bad times, but when I center everything I do around Him, then every tear I cry will water my next dream, and that will become my legacy.

During my final hour before reaching my daughter's dorm, I heard a distant cry in my left ear. I turned the music down to hear it better. It wasn't just a sound; it was a memory. The little girl who used to cry herself to sleep was reaching for the woman I had finally become. "My girl, stop crying. I know you loved living on Bayside because of the wonderful friends you have and how y'all get to play all day, but you're going to move to Florida one day. You'll meet a lot of friends, and you'll travel to places like New York, New Orleans, Texas, Tennessee, and Hawaii. My girl, stop crying. I know you miss your father, but you will make him proud when you graduate college on his birthday."

At that moment, I realized I wasn't just dropping off my daughter, I was picking up every version of myself that had ever felt abandoned. "My girl, stop crying. I know you miss your siblings, but in the future, y'all will have many bonding moments, including a trip to Paris. My girl, listen to me closely. The sorrow you're experiencing in this season is not worthy of comparison with the joys the Lord has in store for you. You beautiful girl, you are the foundation for the strength needed to persevere. On March 16, 2006, you will receive your greatest earthly gift, a daughter. And this daughter will be everything great about you. You will need to teach her everything that your mom taught you, and everything your mama didn't teach you. Once you do that, your daughter will be the curse breaker in your family. She will teach you all how to love and how to forgive. She will be the reason that you turn broken places beautiful."

Reflection: The girl they counted out became the woman they couldn't ignore. The woman I became didn't rise because life was easy. She rose because a little girl refused to stay broken.

Writing Prompt: Write about a time when what was meant to break you turned into your greatest strength.

Picture Gallery

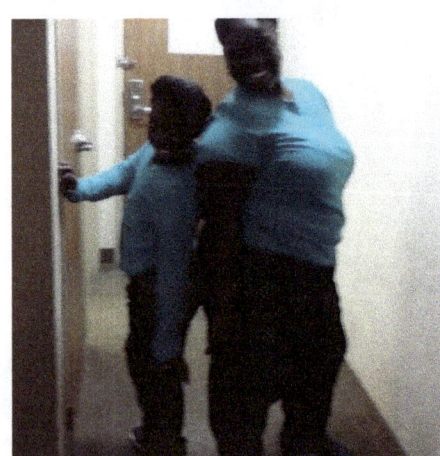

Author Bio

Shawntae Bennett is an educator and storyteller from Charleston, South Carolina, whose journey through resilience and self-discovery inspired her first memoir. Her memoir draws from her own experiences navigating single motherhood, career transitions, and personal healing. With over a decade of experience in public education, she brings honesty and insight to the challenges of balancing purpose and pressure. Shawntae continues to write about personal growth and emotional resilience.

Follow her journey at Shawn*TaeTae the pen* Bennett on Facebook and Instagram:

facebook.com/shawn.tae.tae.the.pen.bennett
instagram.com/shawntaetaethepen/

Email: Shawntae93@gmail.com

www.ingramcontent.com/pod-product-compliance
Lightning Source LLC
Chambersburg PA
CBHW071220160426
43196CB00012B/2352